ZION
NATIONAL PARK

A VISUAL
INTERPRETATION

includes
"TEMPLES of TIME"
an essay by
NICKY LEACH

ZION
NATIONAL PARK

A VISUAL
INTERPRETATION

Cliffs and foliage along the Lower Emerald Pools Trail.

FRONT COVER PHOTO: The Pulpit in the Temple of Sinawava.

ISBN O-939365-36-7 (Paperback)

Printed in Singapore
First Edition 1994

ACKNOWLEDGEMENTS

We would like to take this opportunity to thank the many photographers who made their imagery available to us during the editing of this title. While no single image can effectively replace the actual experience of being there, we believe the visual story told by the images contained in this volume do tell the story of seasonal change and process more effectively than what the visitor would experience while on vacation. On behalf of those who will see this book, we thank you for sharing the fruits of your labors.

We would also like to thank those members of the Zion Natural History Association and the National Park Service whose assistance has helped in the creation and formation of this book—Thank You!

DEDICATION

This book is a visual tribute to the insight of those few who saw the wisdom of setting aside such a tract of land for the future, without regard for personal gain. That Zion and the National Park Service have become models for more than 130 countries from around the world is all the proof that is necessary to confirm their wisdom. We can only hope our own use is consistent with this wisdom and in no way contributes to the degradation of this most extraordinary legacy.

In this spirit, let us all pledge to continue to work, and sacrifice, for the greater good of places such as Zion National Park.

SIERRA PRESS, INC.

4988 Gold Leaf Drive, Mariposa, CA 95338

CONTENTS

ZION
TEMPLES of TIME

by
Nicky Leach

Towers of the Virgin and setting Moon.

INTRODUCTION

Long before you ever reach Zion, the brooding rock giants within its boundaries loom large on the horizon, towering over the wrenched plateaus, pale grass valleys, and fitful human settlements of southwestern Utah. Like a high-walled Moorish city floating in a desert mirage, Zion's snaggle-toothed crags, patinated domes, monolithic towers, and twisted pinnacles seem to rise above the crumbling ledges of the Virgin River Valley like ice cream-colored battlements, watchtowers, minarets, and thrones—an exotic geological display indeed.

In 1880, John Wesley Powell's surveyor Clarence Dutton was one of the first whites to take in the sweeping view of the pristine Parunuweap, Zion, and West Temple canyons from a rare southern vantage point on the Vermilion Cliffs. "In an instant, there flashed before us a scene never to be forgotten," Dutton wrote. "In coming time it will, I believe take rank with a very small number of spectacles each of which will, in its own way, be regarded as the most exquisite of its kind which the world discloses."

As Dutton predicted, Zion has become a magnet for those in search of natural grandeur and one of the crown jewels in the national park system. The park stretches for 229 square miles across the lower reaches of the 10,000-foot Markagunt Plateau, from the high wall of the Vermilion Cliffs through deeply incised canyons, then diagonally northwest over the lava-topped Kolob Terrace to the blood-red folds of the Finger Canyons of the Kolob, where the Colorado Plateau drops abruptly into the searing desert country to the west.

Plants and animals of all kinds have made this park their home. Peregrine falcons and Mexican spotted owls lead quiet, protected lives in remote canyons, and rare cougars still stalk deer over high plateaus. The tiny Zion snail, found nowhere else in the world, leaves its slimy trail among the columbines, monkeyflowers, maidenhair ferns, and water-loving plants that populate Zion's seeping cliff walls. From spring to autumn, the milky trumpets of poisonous sacred datura open nightly along roadsides, so dense in the low elevations the flower is known as Zion lily. Matt-barked junipers and squat pinyons find stubborn footholds in precipitous cliff faces, but cede the higher elevations to ponderosa pines, aspens, and firs, which are better suited to the cool, thin air among Zion's high domes.

Thunderheads swoop in, wreath the knobby temples and buttes of Zion's heartland, and are quickly gone, leaving cascades of life-giving water to spill over the lips of hanging valleys and to stir up the Virgin River into soupy brown-green water. Human presence was once transitory in this rock maze. Anasazi and Paiute Indians came and went with the seasons and raised corn and other staples in the fertile soil along the river, occasionally living beside their fields, then moving on. Only in the twentieth century have we dared to think our role here permanent, as our clamoring for the temples of human

---

The Sentinel, early morning.   8

enterprise threatens to replace those that Nature has wrought.

But this is no mere outdoor museum of rocks, a finished masterpiece; rather, it is a performance art piece, changing aspect constantly, reacting to forces all around it. Earthquakes shudder through the rocky depths, gravity pulls down yet another rock, and water allows life to flourish around waterfalls, springs, and seeps, then rearranges it during powerful flashfloods. Zion is nature's work in progress.

CARVING THE TEMPLE
Converging branches of the small but tuneful Rio Virgin and La Verkin and Taylor creeks in Kolob—all born in the high country to the north—are the master sculptors of the Markagunt Plateau in which Zion nestles. Directly north of Zion Canyon, the North Fork of the Virgin River has worn a groove barely twenty feet wide in places through the 2,000-foot-high pink and white Navajo Sandstone walls, to form the famous Zion Narrows. Exiting these rocky confines, the busy river opens out for a few glorious miles, before converging with its sibling, the East Fork, parallel to State Highway 9.

The abrasive, sediment-laden waters of the river and its tributaries scrape constantly at the jointed Navajo Sandstone cliffs, undermining the precipitous walls, until huge slabs of rock shear away, like onion layers peeling from the bulb. In this manner, the great rocks maintain their verticality, despite persistent undercutting. West of the Kolob Terrace, creeks have incised deep sandy drainages and left bare rock to the mercy of the elements. Persistent erosion fashioned the unusual east-west-trending headlands of Kolob's Finger Canyons and the record-breaking span of Kolob Arch. The sculpting power of water is particularly evident along the fresh break at this far western edge of the Markagunt Plateau, and the hematite exposed in the sandstone is so red that at sunset the cliffs themselves seem to be on fire.

The sheer sandstone faces are cracked, crumbled, smoothed, and polished by falling water, snow, ice, wind, rain, plants, and animals into the landmarks for which Zion is celebrated: the Altar of Sacrifice, Angel's Landing, the Temple of Sinawava, Cable Mountain, the Three Patriarchs, the Watchman, the Great White Throne, the Finger Canyons of the Kolob, Kolob Arch, and many more still in the making. The faces of these great temples range from pale and smooth, to streaked, blackened, bruised purple, brown, and pink, their high coloration caused by the weathering of iron-rich sandstone, miniscule bacteria living on porous sandstone surfaces, and bleeding caprocks on bald summits.

A GEOLOGICAL TIME CAPSULE
The rocky foundation on which Zion sits began to take shape roughly 250 million years ago in an enormous, shallow sea, which covered the western margin of what was once the supercontinent of Pangaea. Fossiliferous Kaibab Limestone in the Hurricane Cliffs at the entrance to Kolob Canyons dates from this era of tropical climate and primitive marine creatures. As the

Navajo Sandstone wall towers over the Clear Creek drainage.

climate dried, a delta was born, where stream sediments mixed with limy marine deposits, and eventually hardened into the soft, colorful bands of the Moenkopi Formation. The Moenkopi seems to blend with the overlying, multicolored layers of gravel, sand, volcanic ash, and petrified wood of the crumbling Chinle Formation rocks in the Virgin River Valley. Uranium is plentiful in the mineral-laden Chinle. It attracted mid-20th-century prospectors, who descended in droves to extract the ore for government stockpiles. The sulphur-colored prince's plume also makes its home here, where selenium is most plentiful.

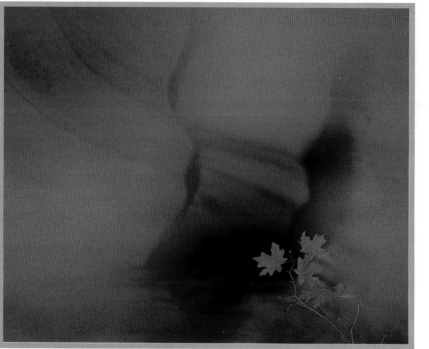

As the continents began to drift apart and the climate changed again, lakes filled depressions and streams cut shallow pathways across the evolving landscape. Freshwater deposits were compressed into the colorful tinted rocks of the Moenave and Kayenta formations, which form compact ledges in the main park. Dinosaurs dominated the earth during this period, their tracks in the ruddy Kayenta Formation a vivid reminder of the time when flesh and blood giants, not stone monoliths, ruled the land.

150,000 square miles of the West. Nothing, not even the Sahara, can compare to this searing hell of blowing sand, which piled into a series of cross-bedded dunes up to 3,000 feet high. In Zion, this cross-bedding is particularly distinctive on the East Rim, where the changing direction of the Jurassic winds and the later action of rainwater percolating down joints in the rock is preserved in the cross-hatched surface of landmarks like Checkerboard Mesa. The fine-grained, loosely cemented Navajo Sandstone reaches its greatest thickness in Zion Canyon's 2,400-foot-high Temple of Sinawava—making Zion the best place anywhere to view this champion cliff-former.

The marine sediments in the Temple Cap and Carmel formations that top some of Zion's best-known landmarks speak of another round of seas that reclaimed the desert a few million years later. Only the remote Kolob area contains younger rock strata: the Cretaceous Dakota Formation that tops 8,766-foot Horse Ranch Mountain, the highest mountain in the park, and basalts barely several million years old that darken the surface of the Kolob Terrace.

THE NAVAJO DESERT

All of this is but a preamble, though, to what came next. For the Zion we know today owes its existence to the period, 175 million years ago, when increasing aridity led the Navajo desert to invade roughly

A RESTLESS LANDSCAPE

The laying down of Zion's sedimentary deposits was mostly complete by about 65 million years ago, and it has been left to ongoing orogenic activity and erosion to continue the work of shaping the land. The

Bigtooth maple and sandstone wall.

130,000-square-mile geological province dubbed the Colorado Plateau began its mile-high rise during this early Cenozoic Era, at about the same time as the dinosaurs disappeared and mammals began their ascendance. One recent theory holds that a meteor crashed into the earth, bringing on a nuclear winter that killed the dinosaurs. Is it mere coincidence, then, that one of the most important mountain-building episodes in the earth's history began to take place around that time? Food for thought, perhaps.

A series of deep-seated parallel faults run across this region. The biggest of these, the Hurricane Fault, clearly marks the edge of the Markagunt (and Colorado) Plateau before it drops away into the low-lying Basin and Range desert country to the west. Movements along this ancient fault line created the contorted Kanarra Fold in Zion's Kolob Canyons, long before the Colorado Plateau was squeezed up. But the high plateaus that seem to float across southern Utah came into existence much later, roughly 15 million years ago, when the release of pressure along faults caused the Markagunt, Paunsaugunt, Kaibab, and Aquarius plateaus to break away and rise even higher on the parent Colorado Plateau (which averages 5,000 feet in elevation). These soaring tablelands have remained distinct entities ever since, their shapes continually reworked by natural sculpting into the steps of a colorful geological "Grand Staircase," which marches northward from the Grand Canyon through Zion to Bryce Canyon. Earthquakes still rumble along this

southernmost extension of the active Wasatch Fault (second only to California's San Andreas Fault in potential destructiveness). Seismic activity causes rock slides, like the one that fell outside the hamlet of Springdale in September 1992. Such incidents remind us that we are standing on a young and restless land.

ALL CREATURES GREAT AND SMALL

Plants and animals have had to acclimate themselves to the 5,000-foot difference in elevation and changing conditions found in Zion. Many of them live in a world within a world, forming unusual alliances with each other and their microenvironments. Differences in temperature, moisture, exposure, and soil allow tremendous variety of species within a narrow radius: cool country Douglas fir across a narrow canyon from desert-loving yucca, lush hanging gardens in wetlands deep in shaded canyons, desert plants atop dry plateaus, and decidedly unstunted junipers in protected drainages in Kolob.

DESERT LOWLANDS

You are reminded that you are in a desert in Zion's lowest elevations, which in the most exposed locations swelter amid 100-degree-Fahrenheit temperatures during dusty summer months. Prehistoric-looking chuckwallas, spinytail lizards, whiptails, and western rattlesnakes live among the sand pockets and slickrock that dominate Zion's East Rim and full-sun sections of Zion Canyon. Desert creatures

Contorted Ponderosa pine atop a sandstone knob in the High Country.

THE GEOLOGIC LAYERS of ZION NATIONAL PARK

CARMEL FORMATION	Fossil bearing limestone deposited on ocean bottom.
TEMPLE CAP FORM.	Clays and silts deposited by floodwaters. Deep red color caused by concentration of iron-oxides. Up to 260 feet thick.
NAVAJO SANDSTONE	Extremely homogeneous sandstone deposited by winds as terrestrial sand dunes, cemented by calcareous secretions from overlying marine deposits (Carmel Formation). Forms the cliffs of Zion Canyon as well as the cliffs and domes of the High Country. Upper part of cliffs are bright tan (nearly white) streaked by iron-oxides from the Temple Cap Formation, lower part of cliffs are pink. For reasons not fully understood the cliffs in the Kolob area are pink from top to bottom. Some fossilized shells and dinosaur tracks. Varies from 1,500 to 2,400 feet thick (at the Temple of Sinawava).
KAYENTA FORMATION	Siltstones and sandstones deposited by slow moving streams on a flood plain. Maroon slopes up to 200 feet thick. Contains fossilized dinosaur tracks.
SPRINGDALE SANDSTONE	Terrestrial sandstones. Pale red cliffs from 75 to 150 feet thick.
DINOSAUR CANYON SANDSTONE **MOENAVE FORMATION**	Siltstones deposited in a marine environment. Some fossilized fish scales. Maroon colored slopes from 140 to 375 feet thick.
CHINLE FORMATION PETRIFIED FOREST	Muds, silts, oozes, and volcanic ash deposited by slow streams in shallow freshwater pools. Fossilized bones, tracks, fish, shells, and petrified wood. Extremely colorful badlands—yellow, lavendar, grey, black, and pink. Up to 350 feet thick.
SHINARUMP CONGLOMERATE	Coarse sand and gravel. Creates prominent cliffs of light tan color. Up to 100 feet thick.
MOENKOPI FORMATION	Narrow bands of sandstone, shale, limestone, and gypsum deposited by streams as well as oceanic and coastal-plain deposits. Marine fossils found in some layers. Banded reds, browns, and pinks. Up to 1,800 feet thick.
KAIBAB LIMESTONE	Marine deposits, top layer of North Rim, Grand Canyon.

VIRGIN RIVER
(Principal agent of erosion)

venture out only in early morning or after the heat of the day has died down. Their movements are dictated, too, by the comings and goings of twilight hunters such as coyotes and gray foxes. Shiny-barked manzanita, sword-leafed yucca, fragrant cliffrose, and rugged serviceberry mingle with dwarf pinyon and juniper and gnarled Gambel and scrub oak in these marginal areas, where exposure to the elements and lack of water is a constant challenge.

Desert dwellers are generally tougher skinned, pricklier, more drought-wary, more opportunistic, and more competitive than other area residents. But tougher doesn't mean less beautiful. Early winter moisture, spring snowmelt, and summer rains allow orange-red Indian paintbrush, deep purple chorispora, neon-colored cactus blossoms, scarlet penstemons, and other flowering species to bloom, giving a zing to the rocks of the canyon and luring insect and bird pollinators that will ensure another year of plant survival.

GARDENS OF EDEN
What is perhaps most memorable about Zion are the many lowland places in which non-desert dwellers manage to live. Step into the narrow recesses and tortuous passageways that riddle these hewn rocks and you may feel you've entered the Garden of Eden.

and damp nooks and crannies along the bases of sheer cliffs. The sandpaper surface of the drizzling rocks is alive with soft lichens, mosses, ferns, and streamers of colorful plants, all of them breathing cool oxygen and well being into the lungs of hikers along the popular Riverside, Weeping Rock, and Emerald Pools trails in Zion Canyon and in moist box canyons, slots, and amphitheaters throughout the park.

Temperatures in these cool canyons may be 10 to 20 degrees cooler than in sunlit pockets. Toads, frogs, shiny dark Zion snails, colorful bigtooth maples, singleleaf ashes, and the musical canyon wren, whose merry downward-lilting song reverberates off the walls, find them perfect hideaways.

Water, which cut these canyons and gives them life, is often close at hand. What passes for a river here would be a stream elsewhere, but few streams can boast such mighty achievements! The riverbanks are home to a tangle of thirsty cottonwoods, boxelders, velvet ash, willows, and the lovely but inhospitable salt cedar, which is quickly vanquishing western waterways. This latticework of greenery is a popular haunt for birds, especially the dipper, which splashes in the shallows. Animals come to drink in off-peak hours, away from nosy tourists. You will need to be up at dawn to surprise one of the shy canyon residents that hesitantly crouch at the water's edge. Bighorn sheep, reintroduced into Zion, are among them, but lucky is the human who catches sight of one of these timid rockclimbers.

Groundwater percolating down through the large pores of Navajo Sandstone finds its passage blocked when it meets the watertight skin of the Kayenta, forcing the water out as springlines, waterfalls, pools,

Orderville Canyon, tributary to the North Fork of the Virgin River.

THE PLATEAUS

It's a arduous climb out of Zion Canyon, but once you reach Zion's rooftops, your narrowed vision changes. A great swoop of lofty plateau opens into waves of scored and striated Navajo slickrock, dressed up with sagebrush, Gambel oak, mountain mahogany, Rocky Mountain juniper, and heavy-plated ponderosa pine. Above 7,500 feet, clusters of firs and delicate aspens appear. To the east, the Navajo dunes seem barely "petrified," their etched surfaces punctuated by gravity-defying pinyons and junipers. Warmer exposures and minimal rainfall allow some desert plants to survive, even at higher elevations—another strange anomaly in Zion.

To the west, a three-day trek across wild highlands takes hikers over the high point of the Kolob Terrace, past lava-covered hillsides, golden grasslands, sheer cliffs, occasional ranches and cattle herds outside the park, and down once more into the labyrinth of creeks in Kolob Canyons. Deep snows close much of the Kolob Terrace from October to April, but it is a side of Zion that no one should miss, if only viewed by car along the steep Kolob Reservoir Road north of Virgin.

The plateaus are home to mule deer and elk, the preferred prey of silent mountain lions and bobcats, although a jackrabbit or cottontail might do. Throaty ravens and large-winged golden eagles make lazy spirals in open skies, while cliff-loving peregrine falcons find the perpendicular walls of the Finger Canyons a safe haven to nest in. Mexican spotted owls maintain a low profile in the most remote box canyons in the park. Lonely and less visited, these high-flung corners of Zion are a place where the spirit soars heavenward, "closest to God," as the Mormon name Kolob describes.

PASSERSBY AND SETTLERS

When the Mormons arrived in the 1850s, native people had been living in harmony with the desert for many centuries. Until they moved on, around A.D. 1200, members of the Anasazi culture had hunted game, gathered seeds, tubers, and other wild plants, and farmed fertile floodplains along the Virgin River. The Anasazi constructed small granaries within cliffside alcoves, inscribed weathered rock surfaces with their cryptic symbols and representations, and built at least one sizeable pueblo near the confluence of the North and East forks of the Virgin River. The Paiutes probably learned crop cultivation from these predecessors and ventured in among Zion's great rocks in search of game and native plants, undoubtedly awestruck by the canyon's powerful presence but increasingly knowledgeable about how it could sustain them. Paiute names have remained attached to Zion: Parunuweap, "canyon with a swift stream of water," and Mukuntuweap, "canyon that is straight like an arrow," John Wesley Powell's preferred name for Zion.

Great Basin Spadefoot toads in a shallow waterpocket.   14

But it was the industrious and oft-persecuted Mormons who placed a lasting stamp on this region. Their neat little farms, well-maintained homes, colorful gardens, irrigation systems, mechanical inventions, rock churches, and meeting halls can be found throughout southern Utah, attempting to bring human order to the desert wilderness. Charged by Church President Brigham Young with colonizing what he hoped would be the Mormon homeland of Deseret, the first missionaries to the area took inventory of everything they saw and sent detailed reports to church elders in Salt Lake City. Young Nephi Johnson, a missionary and interpreter, was led to the mouth of Zion by a Paiute guide in 1858, but apparently recommended other places for settlement.

Biblical Zion. The words of the prophet Isaiah seemed to find their true expression in these sheltered canyons: "The Lord shall comfort Zion: he will comfort all her waste places; and he will make her wilderness like Eden, and her desert like the garden of the Lord; joy and gladness shall be found therein; thanksgiving, and the voice of melody." Looking around, who could doubt him?

CLOSER TO ZION

It wasn't until several pioneering farming families founded Springdale, at the time of the Great Rain of 1861-1862, that Zion Canyon attracted the interest of locals like Joseph Black. Black explored the canyon and regaled people with stories that seemed so overblown they laughingly called the place "Joseph's Glory." By 1863, Isaac Behunin had built a cabin in Zion Canyon and was trying to farm there (roughly where Zion Lodge is now located), along with the Heaps family, across the canyon.

It was Behunin, a Mormon who had experienced more than his share of the slings and arrows of persecution, who believed he had found the

Well, Brigham Young for one was not convinced! After bouncing along the rough trails to the canyon around 1870, he harrumphed that the place was definitely "Not Zion." But even though Indian competition and unsuccessful Mormon experiments like the United Order led to the canyon's abandonment soon after, the people of the region still referred to the canyon as Zion, and some still dreamed of making a living there. As a teenager, local boy David Flanigan had been impressed by a cable that allowed mail to be lowered to Shunesburg from Kanab. At the turn of the century, he decided he could design a similar contraption in Zion Canyon to bring timber from the plateau down into the valley (something Brigham Young had foreseen). Flanigan created an elaborate system of wires and pulleys running down the face of Cable Mountain and operated his cable successfully for a few years. It soon became quite the thing to take the cable, until several unfortunate accidents closed it forever. Traces of the invention may still be seen on Cable Mountain today.

Collared lizard sunning itself.

PARKS AND PEOPLE

But the world beyond Zion was changing, too, and a new appreciation for America's natural treasures was taking hold. Frederick Dellenbaugh and Clarence Dutton, members of John Wesley Powell's U.S. Geological Survey exploring parties, had returned to southern Utah on visits and extolled Zion's praises in their magazine articles and books. Artists and photographers offered the first visual proof of Zion's scenic grandeur to an incredulous public back East. By 1908, Leo Snow, a St. George-based USGS surveyor, had reported to Washington that, in his opinion, "this canyon should be set apart as a national park." No sooner said than done. In 1909, Mukuntuweap National Monument was set aside by President Taft for protection from private development.

Protection did not mean access, though, and the lack of roads was a deterrent to visitation. A dirt track followed the Virgin River to Springdale through the valley from the west, and local rancher John Winder and his neighbors built a rough road over Zion's East Rim to markets and ranches in Long Valley at the turn of the century. The route is now the East Rim Trail. In 1913, Utah Governor Spry visited Zion and began lobbying for better highways to southern Utah's scenic areas. He commandeered work parties of convicts to build roads from Cedar City south to Toquerville and from La Verkin east to Springdale, and local communities also pledged funds to make the region more accessible.

WHAT'S IN A NAME?

Limited access did not prevent a Methodist minister, Frederick Vining Fisher of Ogden, Utah, from riding into Zion Canyon on horseback with several young colleagues in 1915 to view for themselves what they had heard about. Excited by the spectacle, Fisher and his cohorts were moved to name many of the great landmarks in Zion. Riding beneath one monumental rock, Fisher exclaimed: "Boys, I have looked for this mountain all my life but I never expected to find it in this world. This mountain is the Great White Throne." They gave similarly inspired names to the Three Patriarchs, the Great Organ, and other rocks in the canyon.

Horace Albright, the young acting director of the newly formed National Park Service, visited the monument in 1917 and stayed in the newly installed tent cabins of Wylie Way Camp, which operated in the canyon until 1923. Albright was "overwhelmed by the loveliness of the valley and the beauty of the canyon walls and was sure that the area was of national park caliber." On his return to Washington, he made it his business to push for Mukuntuweap to be renamed Zion (which happened in 1918) and to get it made into a national park. With NPS Director Stephen Mather's support and congressional backing, Zion became a national park in 1919.

THE REFUGE OPENS ITS DOORS

The 1920s were a boom time for southern Utah, with tourism growing by leaps and bounds. The powerful Utah Pacific Railroad undertook to build a branch of the railroad to Cedar City and to promote tourism in the area. A branch of the railroad, Utah Parks Company, bought and fixed up the Escalante Hotel in Cedar City in 1923 and acquired Gronway Parry's buses to transport tourists to the parks. That same year, President Warren T. Harding traveled by train to Cedar City and toured Zion, although he was not to survive the trip around America. Utah Parks Company built Zion Lodge in 1925, on the site of the old Wylie Way Camp, and other lodges in Bryce Canyon and Cedar Breaks rapidly followed.

In 1930, one of Zion's most distinctive man-made features was completed: the 1.1-mile Zion-Mt. Carmel Tunnel, which follows Pine and Clear creeks across the east side of the park to U.S. Highway 89, shortening the route between Zion, Bryce, and the Grand Canyon's North Rim by seventy miles and eliminating a dangerous section of mountain road through the Arizona Strip. During the Great Depression, Zion benefitted from construction and maintenance carried out by President Roosevelt's Civilian Conservation Corps, whose work in national parks was of enormous help during a time of cutbacks nationwide.

days. Paved Utah Highway 9 connects to the park's Zion-Mt. Carmel Highway, bridging the gap between U.S. Highway 89 and Interstate 15, the main north-south route between Los Angeles and Salt Lake City. The burgeoning community of Springdale at the South Entrance almost exclusively bears the brunt of serving visitor needs for accommodations, gas, food, services, and entertainment. Food and accommodations within the park are strictly limited to the newly restored and always-busy Zion Lodge.

In 1993, nearly three million people visited Zion, and the numbers are certain to keep growing in the future. In the 1980s, new visitor centers were built in the main canyon and at the entrance to Kolob Canyons, which have allowed the park service to make much-needed improvements in services and administration and to offer arriving visitors an excellent orientation to the park. But Zion is facing many of the same problems the most popular parks face: too many cars on its narrow highway and scenic drive, full campgrounds and lodges, increasing numbers of hikers on the trails and in the backcountry, unsafe practices by visitors that place increasing pressure on search and rescue teams, vandalism, disturbance of endangered species, noise from scenic overflights, and uses of its boundary areas and watersheds in a manner that will make it difficult to adequately protect the resources within the park. If Zion is to continue to be the refuge it has always been, these and many other issues will need to be addressed before the 21st century dawns.

MILLIONS COME TO WORSHIP
The early pioneers who bumped over rutted tracks through the Virgin River Valley would be amazed at how easy it is to reach Zion these

Cliff and bare-branched tree, Kolob Canyons area.

WINTER

Checkerboard Mesa, Winter day.

Frozen waterfall along the Middle Fork of Taylor Creek.

Ponderosa pine cones and shattered ice.

The Great White Throne wreathed in ice and snow.   20

Sunset on the East Temple.

Reflected color on ice and snow in Pine Creek, early morning.   22

Iced branches near Weeping Rock.

Bare Cottonwood branches frame The Sentinel, winter morning.　　　24

Clearing winter storm in the Court of the Patriarchs.

SPRING

Scarlet monkeyflower in Parunuweap Canyon (East Fork of the Virgin River).

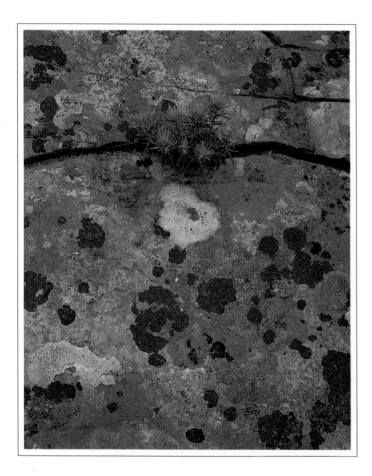

Paintbrush and lichens on sandstone.

Big Spring flows into the Virgin River above The Narrows.

The Watchman crowned with an afternoon rainbow.   28

The subtle coloration of Sand buttercups.

Scarlet monkeyflower along the Left Fork of North Creek.   30

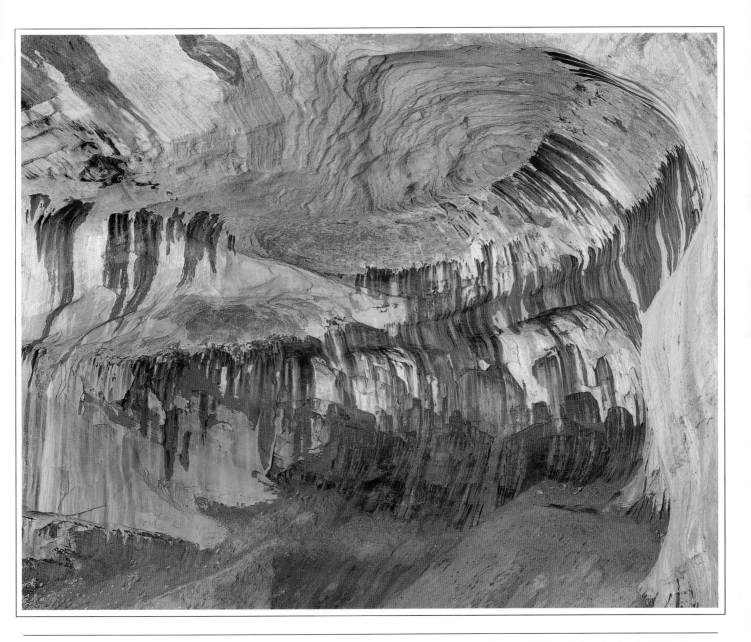

31   Double Arch Alcove, Middle Fork of Taylor Creek, Kolob Canyons.

Fremont cottonwood and waterfall in The Temple of Sinawava.

Weeping Rock against a cloudless sky.

Dwarfed ponderosa pine and cliff at sunset.

Pine Creek and cliffs near the Virgin River.

East Temple at sunrise, Canyon Overlook Trail.

Cliff and tree, Finger Canyons of the Kolob.

SUMMER

Cross-bedded sandstone in the High Country above Clear Creek.

Archangel Cascades, Left Fork of North Creek.

Water-worn slot in Navajo Sandstone.

Deep Creek near its confluence with the North Fork of the Virgin River.   40

White-tufted evening primrose and sandstone wall.

Waterfalls in Heaps Canyon (Emerald Pools area). 42

Prehistoric Anasazi granary within a cliffside alcove.

Cliff of Navajo Sandstone.

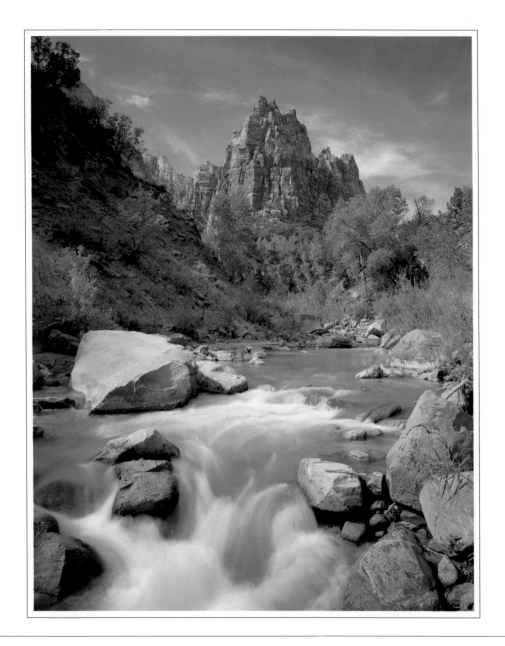

Mt. Moroni towers above the Virgin River.

Afternoon light on Checkerboard Mesa.

The Narrows of the Virgin River.

AUTUMN

Autumn color surrounds a sandstone block.

The Pulpit in the Temple of Sinawava.

Echo Canyon, the East Rim Trail.

Weeping Rock and the Great White Throne.

Maples and Virgin River in the Temple of Sinawava.

Aspen forest near Lava Point, Upper Kolob Plateau. 52

Gambel Oak leaf changes color as Autumn arrives.

Fremont cottonwoods beneath towering cliffs, late afternoon.   54

Maples aflame with Fall color along Clear Creek.

Cottonwoods and the Great White Throne from the Temple of Sinawava.

Bigtooth maple leaf on crossbedded sandstone.

The Watchman, stormy sunset.

Changing colors of foliage bordering Clear Creek.

WINTER
(a brief reprise)

Cliff and pines blanketed in fresh snow.

Angels Landing on a crisp Winter morning.

Snow on crossbedded sandstone in the High Country.

Cliffs of the Kolob seen at sunset from Kolob Canyons Viewpoint.

SUGGESTED READING

Abbey, Edward. *Desert Solitaire: A Season in the Wilderness.* (1968). Reprint. Tucson, AZ: University of Arizona Press.1988.

Brereton, Thomas and James Dunaway. *Exploring the Backcountry of Zion National Park.*Springdale, UT: Zion Natural History Association. 1988.

Bruhn, Arthur. *Southern Utah's Land of Color.* Completely revised and updated by Nicky Leach. Springdale,UT: Zion Natural History Association. 1993.

Crawford, J.L. *Zion Album: A Nostalgic History of Zion Canyon.* Springdale, UT: Zion Natural History Association. 1986.

Crawford, J.L. *Zion National Park: Towers of Stone.* Reprint. (1988). Springdale, UT: Zion Natural History Association. 1994.

Leach, Nicky. *The Guide to the National Parks of the Southwest.* Tucson, AZ: Southwest Parks and Monuments Association. 1992.

Lister, Florence C. and Robert W. *Those Who Came Before: Southwestern Archeology in the National Park System.* Revised. (1983). Tucson, AZ: Southwest Parks and Monuments Association. 1994.

Stegner, Wallace. *Beyond the Hundredth Meridian: John Wesley Powell and the Second Opening of the West.* (1954). Reprint. New York, NY: Viking Penguin.1992.

Welch, Stanley L. *Wildflowers of Zion National Park.* Springdale, UT: Zion Natural History Association. 1990.

The Zion Natural History Association, one of many non-profit organizations chartered by Congress to aid the National Parks, is an excellent source of affordably priced guides, pamphlets, and books. Their publications may be found in the sales areas of the Visitor Centers or by contacting them directly:

Zion Natural History Association
Zion National Park
Springdale, UT 84767

PHOTOGRAPHIC CREDITS

Mary Allen:28.
Barbara A. Brundege:57,Back Cover (Middle).
Todd Caudle:36.
Bob Clemenz:45.
Carr Clifton:Front Cover,49(Left),54, 58.
Charles Cramer: 32,37,55,59.
Tom Danielsen:31.
Jack W. Dykinga: 11,34.
Jeff Gnass:20,46,61(Left).
Robert Holmes:33.
Leland Howard:17,19 (Left).
George H. Huey: 18,25,47,50,56.
Gary Ladd:40,44.
Jeff Nicholas:2,3,8,22,27 (Left),38,39(Right),43,62.
Pat O'Hara: 7,10,16,19(Right),24, 35,61(Right).
Rod Planck (Dembinsky Associates):53.
Branson Reynolds:15.
Tom Till:21,26, 27(Right),60.
Larry Ulrich:13,14,29,30,39(Left), 42,49 (Right),51,Back Cover (Left).
John Ward: 8,23,Back Cover (Right).
Howard Weamer:52.
Jim Wilson:41,48.

CREDITS

"Temples of Time" essay by Nicky Leach
Zion National Park Map by Jeff Nicholas
Edited by Rose Houk
Book Design by Jeff Nicholas
Photo Editor: Jeff Nicholas
Printing coordinated by TWP, Ltd., Berkeley, Ca.
Printed in Singapore, 1994

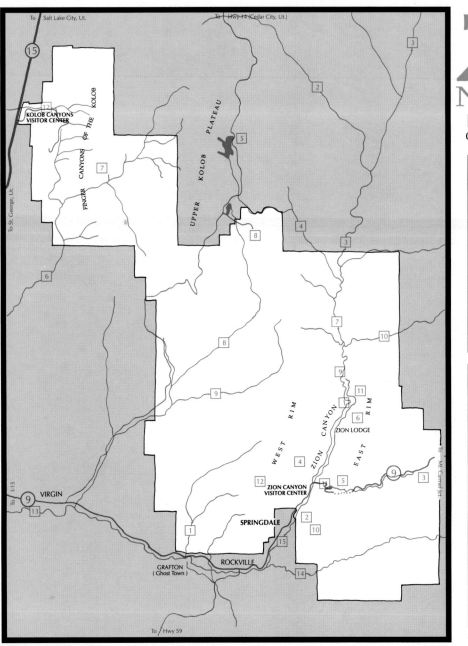

ZION
NATIONAL PARK

0 1 2 3 4 5   10 M

1	Angels Landing
2	Campgrounds
3	Checkerboard Mesa
4	Court of the Patriarchs
5	The Great Arch
6	The Great White Throne
7	Kolob Arch
8	Lava Point
9	Temple of Sinawava
10	The Watchman
11	Weeping Rock
12	West Temple & Towers of the Virgin

1	Coalpits Wash
2	Crystal Creek
3	Deep Creek
4	Kolob Creek
5	Kolob Reservoir
6	La Verkin Creek
7	The Narrows of the Virgin River
8	North Creek (Left Fork)
9	North Creek (Right Fork)
10	Orderville Canyon
11	Pine Creek & Clear Creek
12	Taylor Creek
13	Virgin River
14	Virgin River—East Fork (Parunuweap Canyon)
15	Virgin River—North Fork (Mukuntuweap Canyon)